The Falling Leaf
Does Not Hate
The Wind

Also by D. J. Etchell

Sonnets from the Iliad

Sonnets from the Odyssey

The Lych-Gate

Not to be read by your Wife and servants

Mckinley

The Falling Leaf
Does Not Hate
The Wind

Poems of Death and Autumn

A valedictory collection

D. J. Etchell

Burghwallis Books

First published in 2018 by Burghwallis Books

Cover art by Brian Glidden

ISBN 978-0-9560838-7-6

Publishing services by
Mushroom Publishing Services, Bath UK
mail@mushroompublishing.com

Printed and bound by
Lightning Source

For all those in torment!

Contents

Lost Days	1
Amber	2
The Days of the living	3
Tyre and Trebizond	4
Wild Bees	5
The Lens	6
Life in Death	8
Dreams	9
The Argosy	10
Another Autumn	11
Sonnet to Another Portuguese	13
Cobwebs	14
The Jongleur	15
Life's heartbeat	16
Restless Days	17
Eternities' Soft Breeze	18
Wither the Snowdrops?	19
They Falter	21
The Existential Sine Qua None	22
Alice	24
The Dawn of Nevermore	25
Raw Winds	26
The Torment of a Moment	27
Move On	28
All Hallows' Eve	29
In Celebration	30
As an Eremite	31
The Skyline Burns	32
Demon Midnight	33
The Days	34
A Storm	35

Late Autumn	36
Eulogy	37
Doom-cursed Days	38
My Muse	39
To a Fellow voyager on the Sea of dreams	40
A Reaper	41
Life's Pendulum	42
More Deaths	43
The Days Which are Left	44
Old Colours	45
I Have no Title to these Fields	46
Autumn's Child	47
The Sands	48
Solstice	49
Baleful Demons	50
The Daylight	52
Melancholic Autumn	53
I am the Raggledy-Taggledy Crow	54
The Raging Red and the Pallid Leprous White	55
O'Herlihy	56
A Hardly Noticed Year	57
A Robin	58
Those Last Few Leaves	59
I am the Prince of Darkness	60
A Funeral in Askern	61
I must call forth from Silence and the Night	62
Decaying Leaves	63
A Vessel, Worthy, Old	64
Almost There	65
Blithe Autumn	66
This is the Time	67
Meadow Sadness	68
Blotched Russets	69
Unsubtle Death	70

The Days We Own are Fleeting 71
No point now in regret 73
Beyond the Far Horizon 74
The Wrenching of Death 75
The Last spartan at Thermopylae 76
Swinburneian 80

Bleak Elegies **81**
The Moon 83
Soon You Must Die 84
Liars 85
That Dark Wind 86
Change 87
Demon Bane 88
The B Way 89
Realisation 90
Tattoo 91
Pretty Poems 92
Late Wasps 93
Epitaph 94
Wild Red Rage 95
Evil Things 96
The Raven 98
The Man 99
Sepulchral Hours 100
The Damned 101
A Second Premonition 102
Tormenting Darkness 103

Odes Autumnal **105**
To Autumn 107
To Darkness and the Firelight 109
To the Ending of Autumn 111
To the Eternal Moon 113
To Cynicism 116

To the Lowly Green   119
To the Fading of life   121
To the Early Fifties   123
To the Sublime   126
To Proserpine   128
To the Moon   131
To a Walk down a Country Lane in Winter   133
To the Winter Solstice   135
To Winter Twilight   137
To Winter's Music   139
To What was Lost   141
To the Coming Light   143

Lost Days

Late August arriving, announces the dying
Which follows the solstice with dolorous heat,
Pale grasses drying hymn dirges for summer,
Wind-winnowed fields lie with harvest complete.

Sad stalks of stubble stand, pointed, defending,
Pauper-princed realms once pavilioned in gold,
Tarn-dank mists, descending, drifting, so empty
Wraith-white announcing this year has grown old.

Spring's maenad mad-lusting spring music is ended
That sweet lyre lies silent through darkening days.
Soon swallows must gather then sunwards meander
For moon ruled pale witch-nights bring winter's malaise.

Forlornly, lost lovers so sadly remember
That dark dance of pleasure which drove them insane
Soft-sullen September will silence that timbre,
Its full frenzied measure heard never again.

Charon's craft waits now to carry me deathwards
Through doom's veils which drift across dark Acheron,
Life's fable is fading, fond memories dimming,
Soon gone is the singer and lost is his song.

Amber

From amber realms old poet's words conspire,
To free the pagan in me to run wild
And worship at old altars of desire,
Releasing, to roam free, my inner child
Who with his naive eyes existence sees,
Unfettered by that dullness, adulthood.
The sceptic sleeps, the wary cynic flees,
As I stroll through the splendour of my wood
I drink frail glory as the leaves transmute
To drape October in fantastic hues,
Their riot in my mind death's realms refute
As thoughts of Shelly, Keats, release my muse.
Intoxicating autumn beckons me
To roam its realms a while in poetry.

THE DAYS OF THE LIVING

I grow tired of the days of the living,
Am weary of waiting for death,
Though spring wakes, then days are life giving,
Now, sadness seems sure with each breath.

With what I once was, sadly fading,
That love which was strong—just a dream,
The pains of strong passions evading
Dull embers die with a last gleam.

I linger here ever in autumn,
Though buds wake to drink the fresh light,
Their birthing bids summer sweet welcome,
Yet I rule the kingdom of night.

TYRE AND TREBIZOND

The moon slides through a hole in time to fill the void beyond
To worlds it lit so long ago, rich Tyre and Trebizond,
Which echo with immortal dreams of those long claimed by fate,
Ripped from the screaming womb of now, yet now gets ever late,
Moves on, dissolves, reforms, resolves and then once more is gone
Into those dusty realms which wait to claim us, every one.

Frail beauty and that perfumed lust which captivates the young
Fall sweetly from the minstrel's lips when new-love thoughts are sung.
Ephemeral those fragile words as thistledown in air,
As years pass by all lutes grow still, left silent in death's lair.
So cling this eve to memories of beauty mid life's pain,
Sweet reveries—those ecstasies can never come again.

WILD BEES

Wild bees tumble down my wall
Searching as they pass,
They need a crevice or a hole
To hold their humming mass.

Small and workmanlike they look,
They land and pause and probe,
Much needs doing, pollen-days
Will August's blooms prorogue.

I stand, they whirl about my head,
A moment, they are gone
I cannot aid them in their task
This busy tribe moves on.

I think they must have found a place
Up in the limestone wall,
There, ancient mortar crumbles, cracks,
A gap becomes their hall.

I see them search from time to time
Among the luscious blooms,
For they must busy at their task
To fill their storage rooms.

Does Autumn, satisfaction bring?
For them it means an end!
Does having served, fulfilled a need
Some meaning to life lend?

THE LENS

That lens which late September forms
Brings focus to the mind
To magnify that deep within,
Those needs of humankind.

What passes for the soul revives
When wandering the woods,
There threads of cobweb brush my face
Where morning sunlight floods.

For here stand tall those guardian oaks
And elms and bitter yew
And hollies which must ooze blood red,
Its winter tears are due.

All flowers are gone yet black-blue sloes
Bedeck my hidden glades.
Soon rancid-red and sick-pale leaves
Hang limp as last light fades.

Leaf colours riot in this realm
Prefiguring that loss
Of light, when days grow grey and poor
And all I see is dross.

When all is mulch, heaped damp and dank
With rotting leaves piled black.
I hear All Hallows' awful curse
Dread whispered, 'I come back'
Each year to haunt you, thus for now
Drink in late beauties' days,
Store up their treasure, they must last
Through winter's long malaise.

LIFE IN DEATH

A gentle mist wraps round new breaking dawn
As first light seeps to fill this waking day,
No rosy-fingers here just stillness born
Of mourning, for sad summer slips away.

The woods must turn, October's golden realms
Begin tomorrow, weeks of strangeness come;
Soul searing beauty, senses overwhelms,
We drown in riches, by great dying won.

I stroll with life-in-death through autumn's pain;
Exquisite colours crowd these weeping ways,
Though, finite, shadowed sorrows I disdain
To walk in wonder down immortal ways.

Bardic words still sing, and great odes speak
To those who would this pagan splendour seek.

DREAMS

I dreamt through meadowed summer's ease,
Unique within my mind,
There my other self resides
Subdued by soft-sweet days sublime.

Now through autumn I must glide
I see its burning beauty rage,
And drink the torment of decline
On this last, farewell, voyage.

Marooned then on a sterile shore
I wait for rescue from the gloom,
Engulfed by winter's deathly maw
I sense the blackness of the tomb.

I must await that vassal time
To tilt the world into the light
But now bound by December's chains
I watch the ice-dead moon rule night.

THE ARGOSY

I dream of love, that Argosy of sensual delight,
Which glided slow on silken sails through mysteries of night,
When, soft, the moon from summer skies on daring journeys shone,
With virgin seas to be explored and I immortal, young.

On perfumed sheets beneath the stars I navigated well
To find those ports where wanton needs in luscious maids must dwell.
Those fabled harbours of desire with anchorage to win
Where one might berth and spend long hours to serve the needs of sin.

The wrong word perhaps, denoting guilt or secrecy or shame
Pleasures of the flesh sounds odd for life's sweet oldest game,
That Odyssey of languid love where dark eyed sirens call
Or blue-eyed blonds or wilful reds, the young man hears them all.

Those temptresses, in far off ports, for others are still there;
My barque makes for the sunset now I seek for answers there
Beyond the moon, far past the stars, my soul must soon take flight
I sail youth's Argosy 'lost dreams,' into the endless night.

ANOTHER AUTUMN

Now, that poignant dreaming time
Of fading beauty and decline,
When early mists through dying days
Shade withered fronds down hidden ways.

Full fruiting beauty, gathered wheat,
A sense of life fulfilled, replete,
Of hectic reds and swollen gourds
Shelley's, Keats' immortal words.

Departing swifts, that hint of frost,
A transient sense of something lost,
Dew-strung cobwebs, fairy rings,
Delights the harvest-moon now brings.

Aimless, drifting, wind plucked leaves,
Gale-flung rain against my eaves,
Urgent brooks, which rush to fill
Half empty pool and sluggish rill.

Sudden toadstools sprung by night
Which mulch and wither in the light,
Brown bats flit on leather wing
To steal those moths soft dusk will bring.

Low ivy waits, soon it will rule
With yew and holly, cheering Yule,
Till May's sweet buds in garb, wild green,
Will bright dark winters blighted dream.

Sodden pathways, sullen clouds
Depressed, hung low, October's shrouds
The wood pulls in, prepares for sleep
Bright-eyes their watch through winter keep.

Death's grey bloom dusts berries black
Which with scarlets hedgerows pack.
Near grass forlorn late poppies blow
On barren fields which wait the plough.

A pallid sun through wrinkled skies
All luxurious warmth denies.
Here loss and beauties' gifts combine,
Another autumn comes, sublime.

Sonnet to Another Portuguese

A sonnet to another Portuguese
On that conundrum which arrives each day
From dawn until I take my restful ease,
Till twilight falls, I ponder in dismay
On what we so called humans purpose is:
Consumption and destruction, life must bleed?
Our presence all our brethren damages,
Their sacrifice demanded by our greed.

My only refuge from this madness here
Is found in poems bequeathed by better days
When bards held nature and its wonders dear
Bequeathing splendour in their autumn lays.

A glass of wine, soft twilight, troubles cease
I read the Sonnets from the Portuguese.

COBWEBS

Now, dew-diamond cobwebs form by night
In stillness, for the mists may not yet freeze.
My stout iron gates are home to circlets bright
Bejewelled by imps who spin when no one sees.
Some think small spiders do this work but no!
They are mere guardians of each silken fort,
Who watch by day while elvish hands below
Forge silver strands from moonbeams sprites have caught.
From equinox to late October they
Are busy when the harvest moon is full
Conspiring while the bats and owlets play
To weave and make my mornings magical.
Whenever you see cobwebs thus be sure
Those realms where fairies live must still endure.

THE JONGLEUR

Free and wild I wander—down old paths and ways
The rising sun will wake me—to late autumn days,
As dawn, streaked red as roses—draws mists from the fields,
I'll see before it closes what beauties this one yields.

The robin's song delights me—swallows long are gone,
Like them I drift so freely—until my sojourn's done,
There are no fetters on me—I choose where I may roam,
I minstrel over dale and heath forgoing hearth and home.

White clouds are my companions—they glide and scud in glee,
Sometimes they heap in thunder—or drizzle misery,
The moon at midnight calls me—drawn on by stately sails
Through each still and starlit night that voyage never fails.

I scurry through bright falling leaves—in vagabond caprice,
Oh! would this gay kaleidoscope—of wonder never cease,
Boughs must bend and branches crack—in woods wracked by the storm
Their travails are this season's sport induced where gales are born.

I am your boon companion—recall when we last met,
I left your dark heart filled with joy—and banished all regret,
I filled your world with 'hectic reds'—mind visions which spellbind
That breath of autumn's being still—I am the Wild West Wind!

LIFE'S HEARTBEAT

Life's feeble heartbeat slows,
Pale dawns are veiled in mists
Where crouch poor-wretch hedgerows,
By blight-dark fever kissed.

Now sinks the dying sun
Its cycle is complete.
From spring new life was won
Now harvested, replete.

Soon new virgin snows
Will purify the earth,
While Yuletide cheer allows
A brief respite of mirth.

Now at All Hallows' eve
I seek the log fire's ease
For dreary days conceive
Dark thoughts as pale light fades.

For death, perpetual
Must claim all life in fee,
Our precious years must fall
Erased from memory.

Restless Days

Impatient dawns then restless days bring down unease with dusk,
Moaning winds search round my eaves as twilight falls, sub fusc.
This errant month is cold then warm or filled with calm or storm,
Such agitation marks each week till elvish spring is born.
For wild November's so uncouth, so changeable, I find
It really is the sort of month that can't make up its mind.
In mad March—squalls, in April—showers, then darling buds in May
But chaos now as Northern gales the huddled copses flay.
Then still blue skies, so bright the sun, the gullible might think
That winter's harm will not be done, don't turn your back or blink,
The next time you look out expect a pandemonium!
Discordant days with snow or hail and skies filled, grey and glum,
Or showers, bright spells or heavy gusts which might bring down a tree
Then clumped white clouds which bank and scud across the sky with glee.
At least now Halloween is past, I know it won't be long
Before the nodding violets come and Robin's cheery song.
The musk-rose and wild thyme will blow and then sweet eglantine,
All long to flood these dismal groves made bright with green woodbine.
The equinox comes soon, in joy, then rule the lords of light,
When Puck brings magic to the woods, all human cares take flight.

ETERNITIES' SOFT BREEZE

While days grow still, in thoughts September stirs,
Olympian poets are reaching for their quills
To paint blithe beauty in exquisite airs,
Bequeathing words of wonder with their skills.
Those giants, Keats' and Shelley's souls which saw
The pain of being hid mid soft decay;
Bequeathed to time their visions evermore
Rise fresh in vivid verse from ancient lay,
Of life, sad-sweet, its transience, that fee,
Paid by carefree youth as night descends,
To prompt dark dreams of when we will not be,
In sorrow swathed as final autumn ends.
Our fate, forgotten, lying with lost leaves
Just dust, stirred by eternities' soft breeze.

WITHER THE SNOWDROPS?

Whither the snowdrops which bring
innocence greeting the sun?
Whose weak feeble rays
Now signal short days
Must lengthen for winter is done.

Whither the yellows of March?
Daffodils, low celandine,
Colours of birth,
New life which the earth
Has woken, to drink the divine.

Whither the tulips which come
Brightening April each year?
Recklessly rich
In garlanding which
Urgent life wills to appear.

Whither the bluebells of May?
Subtle and delicate blooms,
Which race through the woods
In broad azure floods,
Night woven on Fay-fingered looms.

Whither the blossom of June
Apple and Hawthorne and Plum
Perfuming warm air
With pollen-rich fare
For bumbling bees which will come.

Whither the joys of July?
Tree-burst in glorious green,
Verdantly gowned
In high splendour crowned
To greet once more midsummer's dream.

Whither the fields full of wheat?
After late August no more!
Just stubble is left
With iron plough's quick theft
Of gold which the rolling Wolds wore.

Whither full summer, now gone,
Slipped into autumn's decline,
Like Ophelia now,
Pale weeds on her brow,
Drifting in sadness sublime.

Whither the leaves which cascade
Drowning those timber tall halls
With bright brocade quilts
Before this year wilts
And dark reign of foul winter calls!

They Falter

The sombre, still, sad splendour of September
In misty silken sorrow clothes the vale.
The long nights come my world descends to slumber
Round weeping glades the ghostly leaves land, pale.
They falter, whither soon, must be forgotten
Like all who've answered urgent life's brief call.
For matchless beauty fades its bloom turned rotten,
The greatest oak, the strongest man must fall.
But first that burning interlude of autumn,
That pause, that stillness, gifted us by time,
Before it claims its own infinite ransom
It pours a draught, distilled from weeks sublime.
Once more I drink, exquisite, fevered days
On paths turned gold, in woods with death ablaze.

THE EXISTENTIAL SINE QUA NONE

I will remain when you are gone!
Unchained yet bound, moving ever on
Through the woodland groves and the secret places,
Past the pools hid from the sun.
Kissing limpid leaves as autumn races
To those barren months where night replaces
All the hope which youth had won.

That hostage, beauty, soon released!
A crone turned Helen, bent, diseased!
Of those thousand ships aged wrecks remain!
Only hero's ghosts haunt battle feasts
Where the timeless sands cover Troy's great plain.
Yet alien bards sing of Hector's pain
His great fame by death increased.

Round countless stars rise great dynasties
Yet see their deeds, mere footnotes, flee,
Leaving lost, forgotten, shards and dust
And pale faded memories.
The great, the least, just shadows thrust
Through some chaos-dream till our wanderlust
Meets its own Thermopylae.

Unimagined hells and heavens wait
Soon gone where planets met their fate
Through great solar flares, in a gamma burst,
All turn meaningless in that great debate
Which will rage to feed the unending thirst
To seek for meaning, by which were cursed,
Till from life we abdicate.

But I will remain when you are gone
Merciless, I move ever on,
I am that tireless stream sublime:
Existential sine qua non!
Have you guessed the riddle which I rhyme?
I am that god that devil, time!
I must bid farewell anon.

ALICE

What can I do? When may I leave?
Life's transience ends as darkens this eve
To wander death's desert, existence has gone,
Worn down by cruel time, decimation has won.

In the room where she struggles no solace I seek,
I feel anger, resentment, her coughing grows weak.
Through stertorous minutes she gasps out her life;
Despairing, I long for the end of this strife.

Wonders, unique in this life-sea we ride
But our wave-surge has gone by the turn of the tide.
What does it all mean? Where will it all go?
Mid this clamour: existence, what can we all know?

The night now is on us, so sombre the light,
Her face looks so weary the soul must take flight.
She would stay though, love for us burns strong in her eyes
What the spirit desires though her frail form denies.

Thus, what can I do, when may I leave?
Before the next dawning, then I may grieve.
The thought of that loss rends my heart down the years
Locked deep down inside me, too painful for tears.

The Dawn of Nevermore

Hints of blue pale-sear this latest dawn
As dark dreams fade into lethargic night,
Who's last farewell Aurora must suborn,
Sleep's soothing shroud dispelled by her first light,
Which swells and grows to glory of full morn.

I leave the realm of terrors far behind,
For archetypes of death live in her caves
Black tenants of that subterranean mind
Who knows ere long we all must be his slaves,
He waits impatient for all human kind.

I drink this vibrant day, for numbered few
Are those remaining to my precious store.
The best are gone, those twilight ones yet due
Soon sink into the mists of nevermore.

Raw Winds

Raw winds presage a winter's emptiness.
Then, always waiting, waiting for blue skies,
And waking buds to end my 'old distress'
And lift that gloom when I philosophise
On morbid realms where fears and dreams of death
Invade that dead of night when phantoms rise,
To taunt me like some tomb-released Macbeth
With threats of loss or imminent demise.
Still months, before the signs of spring are here,
When twilight lingers longer at day's end.
Here last leaves falter veined and browned and sere
For day by day the gods of dark descend.
I wait that pagan signal to the earth,
Of solstice passed, when sunlight brings rebirth.

THE TORMENT OF A MOMENT

In the torment of a moment I saw a Robin die!
Neck broken on my window, so still, with grey filmed eye.
He left the world behind him and its misery to me
And the curse known as existence, from which it now was free

We dull life with diversions, with sex and pointless drugs
Or drown it in perversions or gamble like poor mugs,
We could even try religion with its dogmas and belief,
But the times they are a changing and old myths bring no relief.

We are flotsam on some ocean with no star to guide our barque,
We drift, have little notion of realities which mark
Our paths in restless rhythm as birth-solstice turns to spring
Which summons all those summers, which bright blissful
beauties bring.

But these days are long behind me, are forever, I am brief,
I move through fading autumn with its dying-sighing fief.
We must all obey death's fiat and reluctantly embark
As this Robin, chaos taken, cast into endless dark.

Move On

Move on, move on, you restless slaves of time
And let unsullied hands pick up the lyre.
Depart, surrender, to death's kiss sublime,
Let phoenix-youth rise from immortal fire.

Your day is almost done and soon the night
With endless silence quiets passion's rage.
Though love once ruled through summers of delight
In far off realms there lurked foul winters wage.

With gifted dawns and eventides, now few,
Enjoy their quiet beauty while you may!
Life's spring runs dry you soon must say adieu
When sounds the sombre knell of closing day.

A fond farewell is all we have to give,
As we depart to sail uncharted seas,
All we gain from that last narrative
Are dream swelled sails pushed by a hope filled breeze.

All Hallows' Eve

These are the days of the spirit sighing,
These are the days when you fear four-score!
These are the days when there's no denying
The path that you tread leads to nevermore.

Soon come those times when old joints are creaking,
Soon come those times when you're malcontent,
Soon come those times with brief days fast leaching
From that small store which the fates have lent.

Darkness must come and will all lives cover,
Darkness so sweet for it ends all pain,
Darkness that spectre who like some lover
Gives just one kiss—never seen again.

Once all was light and a young world beckoned,
Once life was bright and could never cease,
Once I was foolish and never reckoned
How precious then was my life's short lease.

Now in late autumn I hear sad sighing,
Sighing of winds mourning months of loss,
Now come last partings—heartfelt goodbye-ings,
Into death's realms must my dreams soon cross.

Forgotten ghosts rise, these are midnight's shadows,
From crumbling mounds where the long years weep,
There you must lie in those gloom filled meadows
Which lost hopes and dreams of doomed lovers keep.

In Celebration

The equinox which ushers sadness in
Is herald to a season, rich, sublime,
When ripeness fills my woods, then Harlequin
Of Autumn dons rich colours of decline.
Then comes All Hallows' eve when tree's bereft
Of all their beauty stand in mourning groves,
And wistful breezes sight for they have left
Midsummer's blue for autumn's weeping mauves.
Yet now in celebration, time fulfilled,
Droop luscious berries round the streamlets banks,
This fruitfulness by nature's bounty willed,
Lies stored against dark winter's days, with thanks
From creatures who from that bleak fast will win
Life's gift until spring's days of hope begin.

As an Eremite

As an eremite of the latter years in the desert of decline
My thoughts turn on, on to other things, eschewing sex and wine;
Well, I leave them behind for a while at least, my spots are hard to change
The le-o-pard is still within, fatigued though and with mange.

I survey the torpid tundra of a chaos'd life long gone
And search amid that wreckage for a poem or some song,
But all I hear is the old refrain and the sad autumnal sigh
Of the long-dried years and the aching dirge of a world about to die.

I watch as sunset's golden glow turns soft, subsumed by night,
Though I've pondered long no answers come to save me from my plight
From that torment caused by the endless wars of the sub-human condition
My legacy is just fractured verse with a hint of erudition.

So, what do I do? Plod on plod on till there is no path ahead!
I could try a cruise, but to be quite frank: I rather would be dead!
I am quite marooned in the stagnant sea of Sargasso-ennui
But this cannot last for the shackle years must break, then I'll be free.

THE SKYLINE BURNS

The skyline burns hell-dusky red,
Last light from day is bled,
In late November: month of pain,
And decline, it can't regain
lost leaf-bright beauty, all grow old,
Till mulch heaped mounds sad corpses hold.
That tenure which they share with all
Of gilded time must heed death's call
Which opens nether worlds, unknown,
Of silence or for dark deeds sown,
To be judged by one who forged their sin,
Or made pure by rebirth, re-begin.

Ennui, black agony
Falls with the dark, tormenting me
As Proserpine I must descend
To death filled halls till winter's end.
The skyline burns hell-dusky red
As last light from this day is bled.

DEMON MIDNIGHT

A silver sickle, silent, scythes
Through ice-skies velvet-black.
There Demon-Midnight waiting lies
For Hell's last seal to crack.
The witch of Endor holds her breath
And phantoms, legion, pause.
They follow their great Marshal: Death!
Are called by eldritch laws
To banish pity, love and peace,
Contentment and pure joy.
Blood-ravening they seek release
Old evils to employ.
What devils will they alchemise?
What dire-delights will taunt?
Now obscene fantasies arise
And my mad dreamings, haunt.

THE DAYS

The days of burning kisses are long gone
From golden summers in a world sublime.
Yet what from love can I now say was won
In times of folly tasting fruit divine?

Then steeds from Eros bore our naked souls
And whips of flame compelled us to enjoy
Those luscious raptures lust's great god controls,
Through carnal nights when flesh must flesh employ.

Do autumn's wonders compensate for then?
Do mellow pleasures any way compare?
I only know, life burned intensely when
We lay entwined long locked in sin's sweet lair.

The year grows old and all sink in decline,
I drank love deep and should have no regret
But oh! to sip once more youth's heady wine!
To taste your lips before my last sunset.

A Storm

A storm is howling, that last gasp
Of this year's heat, it soon must pass,
For 'the great dyings,' all around
Torn beauty heaped on sodden ground
To weave this season's winding sheet.

Soon wrapped in frost that last array
Will wither into sad decay,
With colours leached from dark mulched brown
For summers' garlands must disown
Those, grown sickly, weak.

A calm has come, the anger's passed
Which rocked stout trees with thunder's blast.
Now silent, velvet, creeping night
Drowns my world in soft twilight:
Spent rage and sullen stillness hover.

What remains now? Thoughts and moods,
I ponder as the word stream floods,
I paint a picture of that blast
Which, with passion spent at last,
Leaves like some sheepish lover.

LATE AUTUMN

Grey cloud glides like a curtain at the dawn
Poured down amid the stark-horizoned trees.
Around dank yews fresh-white dense patches warn
That winter's imps soon claw, then burning-freeze
And nip and bite and pinch red fingers still,
But here inside large coals glow bright and warm,
With cheering heat which guards against the chill
Till light returns again and spring is born.
Outside, the world grows harsh for those who live
In secret burrows deep within the earth;
They wait until the sleeping sun will give
New life to those called forth by spring's rebirth.
I see a fox though nonchalantly lope
Along the wood-side, wary, yet in hope.

EULOGY

Just ragged remnants in gaunt trees still blaze,
Late symphonies of colour agonise
As I, wraith like, must haunt old wooded ways.

I tread my solitary route through life's sad maze
Where solemn boughs, lost summers, eulogise,
Just ragged remnants in gaunt trees still blaze.

These citoyens of death in rich displays
Transmute to grandeur, life's dregs alchemise!
As I, wraith like, must haunt old wooded ways.

Spectral wreaths, wind heaped, in wild arrays
My agonies of being exorcise,
Just ragged remnants in gaunt trees still blaze.

In lessons of the leaves each autumn prays
Mortalities brief lease, to catechise,
As I, wraith like, must haunt old wooded ways.

November winds howl through this year's last days
Where autumn's cursed beauty coldly lies,
Just ragged remnants in gaunt trees still blaze
As I, wraith like, must haunt old wooded ways.

Doom-cursed Days

These winter trees are black, devoid of green,
Apart from ivy huddled round old bole,
They flinch, bent by strong gales which always seem
To rush in fury from the freezing pole.
To gift us sleet and snow and frost's sharp teeth
Which gnaw the vitals of each doom-cursed day,
Each miser's light out giving no relief
Until the spring-fresh-skies relinquish grey.

Each winter is the same! What is the point
Of death cloaked months eked out till end of time?
Of dark depressing days set out of joint!
But spring awaits, then darling summer's wine.
I long for dryad-days and wishful dream
Of sunburnt mirth and blushful Hippocrene.

MY MUSE

My muse torments me in these lonely hours
When moonbeams dance on early, savage, frost.
Then, winter's demons have unholy powers
To curse this empty kingdom of the lost.
All hope, all love, all summer joy is gone
My living shade inhabits each day's shroud
New woven from the gloom of Erewhon,
That nowhere land where fealty is avowed
To Death, who rules bleak darkness for all time
And holds the tortured soul's fond memories
As life's lost echoes of those days sublime.
Forever fled into eternities.
These grim days all my golden thought devours;
My muse torments me in these lonely hours.

To a Fellow voyager on the Sea of dreams

To a fellow voyager on the sea of dreams—
Did we leave our mark beyond the tides?
Or did we drift like all those little lives
To merely service some great captain's schemes.

Did we rebel and kick against those rules?
Which lock the dull conformist in his cell
Or did we march too readily, then fell
Into our parts upon this ship of fools.

We two, I think, did mutiny a while
And crying havoc! left staid lives behind,
To try those dangers which wild spirits find
Far up some Orinoco or Blue Nile.

With love and starlight as our only guides
We ventured not too wisely but so well,
Through yearning's tempests where raw passions swell
In secret places where wild pleasure bides.

As old Odysseus, safely harboured now
In Ithaca with comforts won at home
I feel old longings yet and still would roam
New seas with you at some swift vessel's prow.

A Reaper

A reaper stands, a sentinel, beyond the edge of dawn
His shadow mingled with the mists which drape my autumn morn.

He shimmers in midsummer's heat where blithe wheat ripens, gold,
And glides where frost paints icy nights to mark out winter's cold.

Each day I sense him closer, he must soon meet with me,
He travels with eternity and knows our destiny.

He will not speak of sadness and does not promise gain
Just certainty of passage from which a soul might gain.

All who live must meet him, he will not linger long
He knows of that great mystery which our past deeds have won.

He may know of life's meaning or point the path to peace,
Or know the way to other realms which we must strive to reach.

His hands may hold that seventh seal which marks the end of time,
Or hold the key to mysteries which open doors sublime.

As days grow to fulfilment for harvesting, like corn,
A reaper stands, a sentinel, beyond the edge of dawn.

Life's Pendulum

The day was narcissistic!
All the woods were gay
With flourishes and furbelows
In riotous display.

The wild rose pinks ran riot,
Moist frogs were gaudy-green,
Dark adders glided silky-smooth
Reluctant to be seen.

Dormouse-toffs dined heartily
As plenty could be found,
Yet days are willed to shorten
And open winter's wound.

Life's pendulum swings doom-ward
Down from midsummer's high
Though light still floods my glowing fields
I'll soon hear autumn sigh
Of dying mid such beauty
As swallows say goodbye,
Then must umber months of gloom
Once more claim you and I.

MORE DEATHS

Dull cloying desperate grey from early dawn,
Squeezes darkness from fast fleeing night.
Then dismal day arrives with joy stillborn,
Its sadness bathed in melancholic light,
And I propelled by that slow engine: time!
Am tormented by what it means to be,
To drink life's potion, poisoned yet sublime
Of joy and pain, mixed dark by destiny.
I gnaw existence from declining years
Expecting that all dreams must turn to ill.
Consoled by this—at least extinction nears!
To cleanse this dross called life of thought or will
You gods of chaos why be so unkind
My world is ending, yet I'm left behind.

THE DAYS WHICH ARE LEFT

The moon wanders lonely to dawn,
Sad clouds drift like smoke wisps, forlorn!
The days which are left are as bitter as death
The legend of true love is gone.

Harsh, break grey waves from the sea
On—mind-rocks of sharp misery,
Pools which they leave group like mourners who grieve
In some midnight-bleak cemetery.

Of all birds now, Raven is queen!
With bright eyes which glitter and gleam,
Overseeing that feast where the greatest are least
And nightmares are born of hope's dream.

Silence, alone now remains
Our parting's sad tomb just contains
Long dead memories of such sweet ecstasies,
Reviving them causes such pain!

Exeat! How, from such grief
Can I, Hamlet like, dream of relief?
Solved by the pledge of the razor's red edge
A swift stroke could grant me surcease.

Old Colours

A breeze slow exhaled provokes a soft shush
From sad-sullen woods hung dry green,
For darkening weeks into winter must rush
Then leaves give up tenure, to fall.

The world waits in fear as the sun's arc sinks low
Yet the glory of farewell can briefly be seen.
But the wheat field lies stubbled and waits for the plough
With another year lost to us all.

I wait for old colours, that spectrum of death
Which will blaze through October to cheer my demesne,
With the darkness, All Hallows brings winter's first breath,
Then we fall under night's endless pall.

Before those drear days fly rich pennants, displayed
By trees donning hues of decay's nightmare dream,
Such beauty in death as the year grows dismayed,
With last splendour in autumn's great hall.

I Have no Title to these Fields

I have no title to these fields but own the view
Which every year a rich endowment yields:
The sight of glowing wheat beneath a sun
Which cool green threads to purest gold has spun.

To August's harvest I can stake no claim,
Except the joy of seeing rich grain won.
This sates those primal instincts and old fear
Of famine through some failure of the year.

I did not sow, but revel in the sight
Of poppies flaming mid those swollen ears
Where promises of plenty drink that light
Which soon must fade mid misty autumn's tears.

These in turn give rise to wondrous sights,
On Shadowed paths where varicoloured hues
Intoxicate my senses with delights:
Great dying's gift! Which life's sad dream renews.

Autumn's Child

I am a child of the wild autumn gusts,
Of slow creeping mists which cloak early frosts,
Of ripe poison berries which hang burning bright,
Of ice diamond stars in the velveteen night.

I drink in the world of the wistful last sigh
Of that fondest farewell and the tearful goodbye
I am one with the fox of the keen knowing eye
And the small secret wren, hardly seen, flitting by.

I look at the owl with large eyes, watching me
Do we perhaps share some dream of a life which is free?
Do we share that long route which we lonely ones walk?
Into dark cloistered ways which dusk's shadows have sought.

When an angelic moon lights my sad solitude
Old memories rise with my muse, they collude,
To make poems where the spur is just pure minstrelsy
Of the verse, perfect made, in midnight secrecy.

Here, is life lived in death and dark-wild beauty flung
By those late days which race as brief lives reckless run,
Through those dear gloaming months marking autumn's decline
Till a worn heart can rest through last long wintertime.

THE SANDS

Well gaze no more across the sands
Our time has drifted by.
Yet still, grey seas will beat those strands
Where once walked you and I.

Our moon, no doubt, delights the bay
Above black waters deep,
There ceaseless tides forever play
And Lovers' secrets keep.

There, renewed, young love must lie
Where we once joined as one,
In hours beneath that starry sky
Where foolish dreams were spun.

What point is there to mourn lost nights?
Finality claims all,
We lived and loved we reached those heights
From which, through time, we fall,

Which payment claims, in joy and pain,
Unceasing those demands,
Till visions fade, till none remain
Of love's lost golden lands.

We'll gaze no more across the sands,
We join vast nevermore
And leave fond dreams and memories:
Regrets upon that shore.

SOLSTICE

This morning sees that drenching first cool dew
Which tells that summer's jocund rule has passed.
Sad days now come which all small creatures rue
Those looming days with dark long shadows cast,
To wraith-like haunt the wrecked and ruined wood.

But now the world of fading beauty dawns,
Of slow, low-rolling, chilling, first-born mists
When weak sun on its rising, sluggish yawns
As weary of those golden August trysts,
Where wheat was gathered in a golden flood.

Now scarlet vine leaves sear old limestone walls,
Late russets hang for blackbirds still to glean,
Delicious bounty fills my oaken halls.
I could live forever in this dream!
But winter's doom brings berries red as blood!

BALEFUL DEMONS

Baleful demons ride the gale
Then barge at Autumn's stubborn door
And shriek: 'obey the ancient law!'
'Pray let us in,' they wail.

She sighs, 'but I have leave to rest
And drink this dying beauties' bliss,
My lips now seek life's final kiss
Thus, for the grave I'm dressed.

In russets, sorrels, sombre shades,
Which from black trees have blown,
In poison purples lately grown
And danger's reds from my sweet glades.

Go spend your angst on some bleak cliff
And whip the seas to rage,
Let me turn life's final page
And into darkness slip.

The time for turmoiled love is gone
I long for quietude,
Find other sport, do not intrude
Here restful death is won.

Hemlock-dusk sets out the drink
Then nightshade-eve must fall,
Long shadows fill my gloomy hall
As I to slumber sink.

I wilt, I may not come again,
All follow in their time,
Let me enjoy these days sublime,
So few, so few, remain.'

THE DAYLIGHT

Last aching embers dim. This day's light fades,
Like heatless, feeble, candles, burnt away.
November's almost gone, ghost-gloom pervades
And blighted beauty hangs in ripe dismay.

Last fruits are rotten now, those that remain
With tumbled leaves mulch down in corpse filled mounds.
The dying sun, spring's verdant joy disdains
And autumn lies here pale, with mortal wounds.

The desperate hours, those desperate hours have come
When winter's shadows crowd out fading day
Here ice-winds rule, and soulless nights have won
And demons of despair are loosed to play.

The melancholic moon glows wearily,
That fatalist illuminates the dead,
Whose non-existence drifts on drearily.
I midnight-walk with them in endless dread.

MELANCHOLIC AUTUMN

Melancholic autumn why do you always weep?
Amidst this fading glory, sadly sighing.
Is it that this season has old promises to keep?
With sad farewells in this world, richly dying.

Falling leaves remind us of those lives which hurry past,
Oblivious as by time's rule they wane.
Conundrums of existence must lead to death at last,
A final rite for none may here remain.

The deeper soul knows all too well, this is the shadow world!
A place where phantoms flitter, and where dark dreams delude,
We hope when we have passed the gate truth's banner is unfurled,
To show the reason for the pain of life's brief interlude.

Some hold that restful heaven or nirvana wait for some.
Eternal life or nothingness seem poorish bets to me!
The trouble with belief is that its fervent rivers run
Into some parching desert's sands and not some tranquil sea,

All we have is now! Thus, we must ride time's endless tides
Until we sink into unknowing's deep.
Within this season death and burning beauty both reside,
Thus, melancholic autumn you must weep!

I AM THE RAGGLEDY-TAGGLEDY CROW

I am the raggledy-taggledy crow
Untidily flapping through time's endless flow,
Where barren-bare fields all ache for the spring,
For the dark days are on us and cold suffering.

Our flesh is accursed with such red human pain
We know that we end and may not come again.
For that pendulum doom descends and our fate
Is decided; all we can do now is wait.

I soar over earth with such knowing eyes,
Seeking and marking, there is no disguise
You cannot avoid me, death rides on my wing
Expect me there soon for life's last gift I bring.

The Raging Red and the Pallid Leprous White

These are the times when the subtle mist
Greets the gentle golden dawn
As a frail morn wakes, briefly dew-soft kissed,
And a dying day is born.

These are the times of the raging red
And the pallid leprous white,
When black-spotted wraiths fill the dry ditch bed
As the wind-swept leaves take flight.

These are the times when brief beauty fills
My sere aching autumn halls,
When the mind drinks deep of late woods and hills
As this year's dark curtain falls.

These are the times of the last farewell
Of the sad grey turning tide,
Of decaying dreams and the tolling bell
And pale death's last silent ride.

O'HERLIHY

We Mock at death O'Herlihy
Are we not the stuff of youth?
Wild and bold, undaunted,
We have yet to learn life's truth.

We vaunt our pride O'Herlihy
'Neath a blue-forever sky,
On eternal wings our passion sings,
For we can never die.

Tread lightly now O'Herlihy
For we must pick our way
Through those traps and snares the years lay out
Which cause our kind dismay.

Don't look back O'Herlihy,
The only way is on!
The choice was ours, we made it,
It cannot be undone.

We wait our turn O'Herlihy
At the dark forbidding Styx,
Should we ask wild Charon exeat
From our present, irksome, fix?

A HARDLY NOTICED YEAR

A hardly noticed year sinks in decline,
That's nothing special! Years just come and go.
All sucked down by grey Charybdic time,
In chapters snatched from some great shadow show.
As puppets in a dream through endless night
We wander through its maze forever lost,
The foolish young may taste some brief delight
Then groan in bondage at the awful cost.
Important moments pass, peripheralized
While trivial things our precious hours attract,
Until out little span ends, finalised,
By death in payment of life's brief contract.
Why worry on the trials years might endow?
In pagan autumn's beauty, glory, now!

A Robin

A robin hops along the wall
A tiny mote of jollity,
Bright and cheerful seeking food
And I—weighed down by destiny.

He scouts the garden while I dig,
Discerning what my spade sets free,
He does not seem to give a fig,
To live is his philosophy.

This is enough, he lives and feeds
And thus, survives this freezing day,
He views the world so cheerily
Whilst I, far seeing, feel dismay.

He bounds along in waistcoat, red,
He is the soul of utter joy,
A worm will do, a crumb of bread
Whilst I the bleakest thoughts employ.

He shows me something quite profound,
He has no time for misery
And sings of beauty all around,
There for those with eyes to see.

Those Last Few Leaves

Those last few leaves hang, waiting till they fall,
Poor feeble remnants of a fading year
As shadowed dusk enshrouds bleak autumn's hall
They join their fellows, withered, lifeless, sere.
A dullness fills the world as they depart,
To find the void of darkness and dismay
Which holds all loss, old memories chill my heart,
Of those departed long and gone their way
Into that great beyond, that mystery
That hidden journey which awaits us all.
Now charnel winter waits to claim its fee
For time is short, I wait foul Charon's call.
The woods descend to silence and death's barque
Gives one-way passage to eternal dark.

I am the Prince of Darkness

I am the Prince of Darkness, I am the Duke of Gloom,
Phantasms crowd my churning mind and spectres fill my room.

This year crawls past the equinox to meet all Hallows'-Eve
Attendants of high vaulted night command the day to leave.

Where are the songs of summer now, the swallow and the lark?
Those denizens of pure delight now banished by the dark.

The wild west wind has swept this way, untidy leaves are thrown,
Yellow, pale and hectic red, each dons its autumn gown.

Days rush towards that solstice of ill content once more,
For three weeks either side that slough hell opens up its maw.

Foul twilight demons rule that world which withers with the sun
Now shadowed wraiths of mourning rule for nightmare night
has won.

I know this underworld as well as any Proserpine,
Hades presides, our dismal king all through this withered time.

Hobgoblin cold and elvish frost and fairy flakes of snow
Are welcomed to this kingdom where hope left long ago.

From Christmas Eve until New Year, that brief respite of Yule,
Sorrow's gremlins shun the feast of cheery Lord Misrule.

Thus, for a while I sojourn here entrapped in Winter's tomb
I am the Prince of Darkness, I am the Duke of Gloom.

A Funeral in Askern

A funeral! Serious shit you might think!
What was on display? What I saw made me blink.
Though the women wore black they tottered, stood tall
On sharp killer heels, thus proclaiming to all
As they drew on their ciggies—that fashion must win!
They posed round the box as the boys dropped it in
To that hole in the ground where the poor bloke must stay.
Then the girls grouped above, without much delay
With stiff-legged short paces tip-tapped to the wake
And with gimlet side glances marked down the mistake
Of those who attended in sensible shoes!
The nub of this matter, and these are my views—
Death's incidental to the female race,
But a fuck up in fashion's a lifelong disgrace!

I MUST CALL FORTH FROM SILENCE AND THE NIGHT

I must call forth from silence and the night
Dark dreams which torment, crucify the soul,
Those swirling doubts, dread insights which take flight,
Attempting to give meaning to the whole
Of strange existence on this tiny world,
Which acts as our oasis in the void,
Green mantled, life abundant, snuggly curled
About our star sustained, not yet destroyed,
That life thread down vast aeons hanging on
Until we came, small beings, self-aware
At last, with inklings how our place was won
Upon this orb so cruel yet so fair.

Amid the chaos, order, perhaps some plan
Pervades the cosmos and those quantum realms
Providing insights perhaps to spur on man
To higher beauties till truth overwhelms
To gift poor seekers meaning to this life,
Beyond old myths and fables which still bind,
For some lost in the darkness they suffice
Yet, can we join the angels, humankind?

Decaying Leaves

Just sadness! Dark mulch piled on frost hard ground,
These corpses, sodden, leached of life, dark browned.
Lost remnants of those fleeting pennants high
Vibrant green and noble, now disowned.

Now mundane remnants of foul autumn lie,
Corrupted by low spores, they putrefy,
Withering slowly bathed in winter's sun,
Ice breezes round their grave mounds sadly sigh.

The cycle turns forever, what is won?
What was lost, what alteration done?
As bud filled seasons endlessly repeat,
Then fade to lie with death's great echelon.

A Vessel, Worthy, Old

The craft moves west
Its sails turn gold,
It is a vessel, worthy, old
Which drifts into the night.

Old Sol's half-set
I make slow way,
This breeze is slight at end of day
From which I now take flight.

Last kiss—the rim
Now meets the sea,
I move propelled by destiny
To realms beyond the light.

What waits out there?
Ten trillion stars
With planets stranger than red Mars
New wonders, infinite.

What calls,
Some purpose unrevealed?
Great mysteries by time concealed
Far past a last midnight.

Time's tensors warp
My dreams dissolve,
In ending, which all hopes absolve
When death must life requite.

ALMOST THERE

There's a strangeness in the season
For an ending has begun.
We are waifs bereft of reason,
Is our journey lost or won?

Now the twilight's malefaction
Soaks the heavy evening air,
Do we leave with satisfaction?
Do we exit in despair?

My friend, the road we travel
Lies open into night,
There is much still to unravel
But the steps I take are light.

With nocturne nineteen playing
I would greet death with delight.
Who would linger here dismaying
When a wild soul longs for flight.

BLITHE AUTUMN

What point when passing time dissolves all days?
Dark realms of chaos claim all what was done,
Releasing thought and being from life's maze,
Ending fond delusions of love won.
Blithe autumn's here, existence is so sweet,
Yet seasons come and go like feckless winds.
We reach for more, but none can be replete
Till this brief feast of hours in darkness ends.
It waits now in the shadowed eventide,
Concealed by dawn's soft mist it bides its time,
Till midnight comes that missive is denied,
Death's invoice, which must end life's dream sublime.
Keats' vision comes again, why speculate?
I drown in beauty careless of my fate.

This is the Time

This is the month of the turning leaves
And wind whipped whorls of the fitful breeze,
First the sycamore with its black-blotched rot,
Then the gnarled dry brown of the horse-chestnut.

Lisps the dead-choir song of those soon to fall,
'We await our fate, it must come to all,'
Hanging yellow-pale full of pallid blight
Or we burn with plague-red fever, bright.

This is the vale from which none return,
Now our season ends and for death we yearn,
Passing on from this dream into mystery
As our life-bright years turn to history.

We are born and exist but the gift is brief!
When we leave we may take some small hope, belief,
Who can know? Who can know? We drift down to end
Into endless halls where all souls descend.

MEADOW SADNESS

Across the meadow-sadness drapes this day
As though this languid month had lost desire,
So still the air as cloaks of creeping grey
Dress autumn's mood in mourning's sad attire.
Ennui, loss and all life's worries vie
To fill my mind, for pointlessness is all,
Doom's palette paints my world from earth to sky
All colour blanked out by its deathly pall.
Just yesterday my wood with magic hues
Cheered me as I trod each vibrant glade,
But veils of sorrow now these dark trees choose,
As spectres from a ghost world they're displayed.
Black shadows formed from winter's woes contend,
Will night without a dawn these torments end?

BLOTCHED RUSSETS

Bedraggled trees, kissed white by that first frost
Which ushers in ice-blues of this fresh dawn,
Greet late October where all hope seems lost
For darkness seeps into this world forlorn.
Gloom-days with velvet nights concatenate
To chain my bleeding woods with discontent
For fear and hunger, death and bleakness wait
Until the gods, with spring's first light relent.
Blotched russets hang, full flavoured, lush and round,
I pick them adding to my winter store,
New windfalls strew their bounty on the ground
Where bright eyes feast for now through days unsure,
For what will come, the bitter-cold cruel hell?
Poor un-borns, sleeping, wait, all may be well.

Unsubtle Death

There is no subtlety when life must end!
No death in part, or to some slight degree,
No second chance, to Styx our path descends,
Where wild eyed Charon waits to claim his fee.

The world goes on, a pallid vicar drones:
'In sure and certain hope,' would it were so!
Life's debt is paid, I feel within my bones
Eternal truths no man or faith can know.

Then light relief, with distant cousins seen,
With food and drink and some fond memory,
Yet inwardly I ponder, what has been
And what awaits in vast eternity?

The Days We Own are Fleeting

The days we own are fleeting,
All love must turn to dust.
Though what we're left is gladness
Bound up in parting's sadness
For time must bring an ending
To silken nights of lust.
The days we own are fleeting,
All love must turn to dust.

We merge with fading shadows,
Wild dreams forever lost.
Our twin and wilding passion
Drunk deep till dawn's light, ashen
Decreed that flesh must sunder
For pleasure's hours must cost.
We merge with fading shadows,
Wild dreams forever lost.

We drowned in delectation,
The nectar of the damned.
Enslaved, bound in possession
Whipped to such heights each session,
With ecstasy as plunder
And need by ardour fanned.
We drowned in delectation,
That nectar of the damned.

Through carnal torment's longing
Bound by red rapture's pain.
In dialogues forbidden
We reached love's mad heights, hidden
From all but those who must,
Forsaking guilt, make claim
Through carnal torment's longing,
Bound by red raptures pain.

What point regret and sorrow
Or seeking death for rest?
We charged into love's battle
Became each other's chattel,
Then slaves to emptiness,
Damned by that lost conquest.
What point regret and sorrow
Or seeking death for rest.

I know there's no returning,
Our time is almost past.
Yet could the seasons falter
Return me to love's altar
And hold me there in thrall,
But love has breathed its last
I know there's no returning
Our time is almost past.

No POINT NOW IN REGRET

With carriages decaying—your train is towed away, just rusty scrap.
The Hounds of Hell are baying—telling you there is no turning back.
A brass band on the platform—welcomes eager souls who must arrive
Yet for the poor departed—there is just this final silent ride,
Into that great unknowing—to that sea beyond all endless seas.
Death's restless tides are flowing—does grim Charon still claim
ferry fees?
Will torment end at Lethe—does some other realm in shadows wait?
Beyond this awful journey—to that place beyond life's closing date.

You curse the pale conductor—but your one-way trip has been reserved,
Your single ticket takes you—to that vasty terminus deserved.
Some promise five-star passports—to those airy kingdoms in the clouds,
And not just feasts for maggots—amid forgotten cerements and shrouds.
The truth is, we are clueless—does some golden ledger list our sins?
Do imps of chaos mock us?—Entropy, confounding order, wins!

Whenever and whatever—life moves only one way down the track,
Its record penned forever—prayer no single letter can redact.
When our deeds are tallied—are we left in surplus or in debt?
Sit back now, say fuck it!—there is just no point in last regret.

BEYOND THE FAR HORIZON

Beyond the far horizon there waits a different sun
Which bathes the dusk with beauty when turmoiled life is done.
Beyond the far horizon I hope for gentle rest
As twilight falls to greet me there must end my quest.
Beyond the far horizon I'll take forever's ease
Enjoying endless summer with its gentle shade and breeze.
Beyond the far horizon there is no fear or pain
Just that quiet contentment good natured hearts may gain.
Beyond the far horizon I'll meet my dogs at play
I know they wait to greet me at the ending of my day.
Beyond the far horizon there are no fires of hell
No abyss filled with darkness where twisted souls might dwell.
I do not think to meet them, they fill that vale regret
They did not choose the human way, thus they may not forget.
Beyond the far horizon lies whichever way you choose!
Choose well in life for death will come and you have much to lose.

THE WRENCHING OF DEATH

The wrenching of death at the fading last sun,
The ending which waits for the time now has come
When the grieved heart must beat like a funeral drum,
Then the moment arrives, all is lost, and all's won.

Then, goodbyes must be said for a light leaves our dream
To move to those realms where bright beauty is seen,
Where the ripples of being must endlessly stream,
Where I feel a good soul might its bounty redeem.

Though, Death is the lord of us all!
Its rule just extends to mere bodily things
Beyond it I feel unimagined truths call,
I wait to discover what ending's gift brings.

THE LAST SPARTAN AT THERMOPYLAE

In Memoriam
Michael Peter Bownes

Time's pulse slows where day meets night
As comes that final faltering light,
The candle dims for death is here
His shadow cloys the living air.

I wait my turn for all are gone
Those gods of youth so wild and strong,
Immortal for a time we seemed,
So long ago that dream was dreamed.

Fierce and proud, hard warriors all,
They rose to answer life's strong call
Thrown its challenges, they won
Each contest till that final one.

I hope Valhalla keeps a place
For me, I would not those disgrace,
They dwell now in that far beyond
Where honour greets those of the bond

Of friendship, of the valiant, proud,
Of those who fought life's fight unbowed,
Not for them the ways of guile
The broken vow, the fawning smile.

As Achilles with Patroklos
I taste that bitter draught of loss.
My comfort comes through seething rage
In silent grief beside the grave.

Life's grey tide turns on time's strand
And all submit to its command,
I feel its current urge me on
And truth be told, I would be gone.

It seems that I remain the last
Of those that darkness waits to grasp,
That last Mohican now alone,
I wait on death to bear me home.

If any gods are there be kind
And loose those bonds of years which bind
Me to decline till wracked by age,
A footnote on life's final page.

Dishonour falls on those who choose
The razor's edge or hemlock juice,
Like Spartans at Thermopylae
I'll fight till life is torn from me.

Socrates, spoke of his fear
Of limp self-pity's empty tear
Better hemlock, then depart
Than eke out days with coward's heart.

Old custom fail, but, yet a few
Are to old steadfast ways still true.
The mass will sell their souls for crumbs,
For baubles, yet their hour still comes.

My friends live on in memory
In private brooding thought, with me,
My soul is mourning, all are gone,
I wait their call to journey on.

The world turns desolate and old
To endless winter filled with cold.
I ponder at dark Lethe's edge
A vassal to my friendships pledge.

Fate and circumstance combine
In some to form the rarest wine,
A vintage pressed from perfect years,
Just dregs remain and parting's tears.

I must serve while I have breath
Their memory this side of death,
They trod that road reserved for those
Who have stout hearts where courage flows.

I hope to follow, follow soon,
Like Lancelot I crave the boon
Of exeat from sullied days,
Release from craven doubts and ways.

Yet for a while I must remain,
My lot requires that I sustain
That oath we swore with words unsaid
A code which binds till all are dead.

Poems of mourning hymn the best,
Keats, great Hector and the rest,
Now let the minstrels string their harps
Another to their ranks embarks.

Receive him maidens of the north,
Serve him as befits his worth,
Fill his beaker to the brim
In that hall where heroes sing.

Given a choice that's where he'd be
Carousing through eternity.
The long ship sails beyond life's end,
Farewell, and journey well my friend.

SWINBURNEIAN

I lived for a moment in a house filled with pleasure
Where sybarite riches drowned the long day.
Inexorable time revealed that this treasure
Was transient dreaming, wrapped in dismay.

For time is eternal and mocks feeble leisure,
Love's feckless foibles and shallow conceits,
For merciless minutes mark out and measure
The end and that parting which all hope defeats.

Yet the hounds of spring are on winter's traces,
Pawing, so eager this season to meet,
For the mother of months fills old shadows and places
With the oldest of urges which new blood will greet.

BLEAK ELEGIES

THE MOON

The moon is the colour of death tonight.
I feel cold fingers clutch my heart.
Time dissolves life's feeble dream.
Perhaps this autumn I'll depart!

Slithering days crawl to their holes
Which open at the edge of night
And then let loose those midnight ghouls
Which gnaw my sanity, till light.

Winter's chill has come so early
Frost licks leaves, sad reds and golds
The lyric of life's song grows dreary
I'll see what non-existence holds.

Soon You Must Die

Soon you must die, there's no escape!
Those thoughts hide mid the shadows in your mind,
You visit them in night's sardonic dreams,
Foul visions rise unchained on midnight's hour.

You know too much of what must then occur
As metabolic pathways choke and fail
And lysosome release lets rigour in
Then death's grey pallor cloaks life's vital form.

The armour of the rational can't deflect
The poisoned painful rapier of death
For you it ends in nothingness alone.
Stars decay to cinders in the dark,
Slow entropy consumes eternity
Till all is done and thought exists no more.
Are they only fantasies or lies?
Those heavens dreamed on trillion feeble worlds?
You will never know, you soon must die.

LIARS

See those smiles, like snakes round Satan's throne!
Inviting, they invite you, please come in!
Into those dark delusions which they spin
From subtle slight omissions and slant words.
Not blatant Goebel falsehoods, but in sum
Evasive constructs crafted to delude.
They come by night, why can't the admass see?

They are fodder, ciphers that is why!
Just cogs in the machine, designed to turn
Un-questioning locked tight within the thrall
Of poor permitted dreams, they must kow-tow
To promises of what their lot might bring.

Thus, just accept your meagre share till death
Removes your cost, that burden to the state.
The taxes raised are spent on better things,
Like we who toil to keep you in your place
Enjoying life's full fruits as media queens
We smile at you like snakes round Satan's throne.

That Dark Wind

That dark wind death, with mournful tone,
Is sighing round my eaves.
'The way is lost your time has come,
I gather in life's sheaves.'

Sad murderers express their will,
It seems religions must
Give licence to the need to kill,
Releasing their vile lust.

Machines improve, our savage ire
Grows better by design.
How soon will Hell's sweet cleansing fire
Us to our end consign.

I feel a sense of coming doom
Grow greater with each day,
Wrecked towns, new innocents entomb
As war's wild furies play.

The list is long, there will be more
Until this race so damned
Is ushered through extinctions door
By some mad waiting hand.

CHANGE

The days are not as they once were in time,
Wild bees are dying all the world seems sad.
But this is autumn, should I be surprised
For changing colours sear into my mind,
Shelly's hectic reds, oh voice sublime,
With melancholic Keats your subtle twin,
The beauty of your age lies withering
Now all your youthful world grows old and sad.

'Where are the songs of summer,' where are they?
Eternal winter waits, they may not come!
The soulless ear avoids the skylark's song,
It may remind of beauty passed away,
Of o'er brimmed vessels, innocence at play!
Of youth's wild days when all the world was glad,
Before ideals and joy met now's decay.
Visions, dreams should not here linger long,
These days are not as they once were in time.

DEMON BANE

This year seeps out, leaves mourning's dregs,
Leached light grows ever pale,
Beggared tree's green gown's turn rags
Hard ravished by this gale.

With sallow cheeks sick autumn comes,
November's curse brings gloom,
A dark existence through life runs
And draws it to the tomb.

So early this year comes despair
Its demons drop their bane,
The fates mark out the doomed, beware!
You may be one they claim.

THE B WAY

Bukowski's way has proved to be so right
About distractions from the coming night,
Slow horses, booze and women occupied
His time away from writing till he died
Of cancer, two packs daily, of that shite.

Sardonic Guru! We should take his lead
As our sad dreams and vanities, we feed,
He stuck his fist right up convention's arse
Broke all the rules, he thought life was a farce
But something deep caused his dark soul to bleed.

Like him
I'd like to try a black and drunken whore
Three hundred pounds of pleasure, screaming MORE!
With moist inviting lips between those open hips
Where sordid-sinful-honeyed pleasure drips
For those who pay as they walk in her door.

I'll maybe write a book or two in time
Or squander dying days in search of rhyme.
Bukowski wrote it neat, just as it came
A cynic, not quite mad and not quite sane,
You need that touch to hear the muse sublime.

REALISATION

The prison ship of life sails ever on
Across the ocean of deluded ways,
Till stopped by death's bleak reef, then you are gone
Into that nowhere world which claims all days.
The Cynic prophets influenced my youth
Which was by Nietzsche, Russell strongly swayed,
I later found that none had grasped the truth
But glimpsed the nightmares man's conceit had made.
The hour is late now, welcome comes the night,
Sunset falls and soon a sleep is won
And dreams of that last fading of the light,
Then gentle rest with all my worries done.
All journeys end, all destinies are thrust
Into time's mists as long forgotten dust.

TATTOO

With chips and gravy finished, greedy-gorged
Then papers screwed up tight in angry scorn,
Discarded, cast off from an empty life
To join the soggy butts upon the floor,
She mouthed into her mobile, something crude,
Then laughed and lit a needed cigarette,
A tattoo in Chinese defaced her neck,
From the Tao perhaps, or just Fuck Off!
I realised that finally I'd met
A woman made of flesh and not of dreams
I christened her 'The Lady of Garrotte!'
She lived it, sucked life dry with no regret,
Expecting nothing from a crap filled world.

She smiled, I smiled, a kindred spirit there
She knew, I knew, and though from different worlds
What we felt of life was much the same,
Philosophies transcending pointless words,
Summed up concisely by her blue tattoo.

PRETTY POEMS

Oh, I can write the pretty poems alright,
Soulful sonnets, dreams of nevermore,
Woods in autumn, stanzas of delight,
But now my muse demands I write it raw!
For disillusion crowds sub-human ways,
The murder-paths are full, it never ends,
Mad politicians plan our 'final days'
Into the pit our so-flawed kind descends.
In that Hell where demons wait in fear,
In trepidation lest we join their kind,
For they know what waits when we come near,
What horrors dwell within the human mind.
The record shows we torture, rape and kill,
Year on year and never have our fill.

LATE WASPS

Late wasps feed on ivy flowers
As chill winds sigh and call
They have not long mid autumn's hours
Before the first frosts fall
To claim them for that multitude,
The ranks of endless dead
Poor victims to vicissitude
As light from day is bled.
Soon subfusc shadows claim the wood
And free their nightmare realm
Where witches roam and chill the blood,
Where dark thoughts overwhelm.
For winter's come and years pass by,
Which all our hopes devour,
Soon with the fallen leaves you'll lie
In yesteryear's dark bower.
In innocence the late wasps feed,
For them this time is good;
Existence, to obey life's creed
Suffices, as it should!

Epitaph

Above me glides the lonely moon,
This autumn demon haunts me still,
Deathless, drifting with no will
Or thought through existential gloom.

Eternal forests of the night
Hold nightmares for the mind aware,
Their shadowed groves hold, loss, despair
And only thoughts of death, delight.

This Earth grows restless now I feel,
Our tenure in this place must end,
All routes to nothingness descend
With no way back or last appeal.

Will Hell's gates open late or soon?
What memory will ages keep
Of mankind, in eternal sleep?
What epitaph will grace our tomb?

Wild Red Rage

As wild red rage of sunset sears my sight
Strange solace in that moment I can find,
As dying beauty ushers in the night.

A vision from the gods for my delight,
A moment's respite from sad humankind,
As wild red rage of sunset sears my sight.

A year is fading, autumn days take flight,
Soft joys of twilight for a while spellbind
As dying beauty ushers in the night.

Death's angel comes to end man's awful plight
Our evils multiply, yet most are blind
For wild red rage of sunset sears their sight.

Vile deeds are done, then come those words contrite
Our brothers die through greed and lies combined,
As dying beauty ushers in our night.

Descending darkness banishes all light,
We soon will lie un-mourned far out of mind,
Yet wild red rage of sunset sears my sight
As dying beauty ushers in the light.

EVIL THINGS

Twilight ushers in such sad times,
Autumn's last days I abhor
'Evil Things' in robes of sorrow
Wait beyond life's closing door.

Light is fading, nature's dying,
Halloween's dark hours implore
Feeble glimmers of dawn's first glow
Frugal, faint, to cross my door.

Ending that black reign of midnight,
Which must be by eldritch law,
Through this season, death delivered
Seemingly for evermore.

Sombre shadows leach each last gleam
Sooner than on days before,
Solstice waits when light's pale slivers
Barely peep through mid-days core.

Ghastly garlands by graves wither,
Nightshade and pale hellebore
These in silence guard each brother
Wrapped in cerements and gore.

Serpent-weeks down time's path slither
Slow to Styx's empty shore,
Charon's from his toils delivered
By fools who now believe no more.

Dreams and hopes descend to Lethe,
Disappearing at its maw.
Friendship's faded, love's forgotten,
Now last dregs from life I pour.

This poor vessel, empty, shrivelled,
Vanished that bright youth we wore,
Lightly then, it seemed forever.
Its rapture nothing may restore.

That sweet seductress, Death, is waiting,
Come to me you lovely whore!
Let me taste your lips with pleasure
Then from all life's pain withdraw.

The Raven

That Raven darkness falls and through its curse
All hope and warmth and beauty are consumed.
Existence exudes pain in thoughts perverse
As joy in life with lost light is entombed.
These are cankered months of mouldering ways,
When cautious life must seek, with desperate need,
Slow routes to summer while this world decays
From plenty into autumn's frugal feed.
While they sleep he haunts harsh winter's lair
To feed on carrion memories which arise
And wraiths of long lost dreams, dressed in despair,
Whilst sanity's thin thread thoughts tyrannize.
The time of dread comes earlier this year,
I drink death's absinthe, pale, from despond's mere.

THE MAN

The gaunt featured man looking very severe
In a tone beyond pity or time,
Said, I swayed feeling dizzy and queer,
'You will be dead soon,' the unfeeling swine!

Doctor Death, it was he! When did he come?
Who made that appointment for me?
Though life's not forever I would like it long
Very long and as long as can be.

He looked rather seedy in Tebbit-brown suit,
His hair lank and greasy and thin.
He said book your place as death's latest recruit,
With headstone and hearse, you begin!

I awoke, I was dreaming and yet from that day
Those words and that scowl haunt me still,
I've lingered a month and to my dismay
I have not completed my will.

SEPULCHRAL HOURS

My bloodless spectre sinks beneath the grey
Of bleak mid-winter's foul, dank, mist draped shroud,
Where pale light seeps through misery of day
Where doom-filled thoughts as wretched torments crowd.
This time consists of death-thoughts, what can shrive
Our sins? I wait that gift of endless sleep.
At night I wander Hades bare alive
Till dawn from demon-dark at last may creep.
Distant spring, your touch will warm the earth,
Through April's gate will pour the sunlit hordes,
Life's torrent in green wildness will rush forth
To cleanse the gloom left by these solstice-lords.
Sepulchral hours your banishment is near
One snowdrop flower will end my world's nadir.

THE DAMNED

Twilight will fall, you will draw your last breath
As the river of time meets the ocean of death,
Here the struggle must cease for the journey is done
Do you wonder what waits past the last of the sun?

The dark breeze will whisper that Lethe is near,
You will meet, wild eyed Charon, all's done have no fear
For you win sweet forgetting, all pain left behind
As the grey of unknowing fills caverns of mind.

For some a foul curse claims a person who lives,
The fog of extinction a bleak bounty gives,
They inhabit dark Hades this side of the Styx,
Those damned, the demented which random fate picks.

The black craft awaits I will stand at the prow
As I ponder this journey I make a last vow.
I'll see and think clearly till comes that last day,
Let wild thoughts burn in me while life-force holds sway.

A Second Premonition

I went past a solid oak door,
I looked through a window's wire mesh,
A coffin stood there, what a bore!
Flower strewn, it contained some poor wretch.

I turned then to leave but the door
Had vanished, I panicked, inside
A small room of wood with walls four,
I was the wretch who had died!

I awoke with a jolt at first light
Glad to enjoy Dawn's rose gleam,
But so vivid, I shiver with fright
Did I wake or is this death's last dream?

Tormenting Darkness

High in the sky hangs the palest of moons,
Its snake silver beams try to enter my rooms,
But my windows are poisoned, they wither and die
Then shrivel to dust with one last wistful sigh.

They journey from crescent, then half, then oblate,
From full they are launched, but all meet the same fate.
Their parent burns cold with a silvery fire,
Malicious, aflame with such deadly desire.

It mocks, you are mortal and numbered your days
Whilst I am forever, in orbit always,
Why bother prolonging, have courage, depart!
To slice the carotid needs so little art.

I am sun-secundus, I furnish drugged light
To fill with dark dreams all the creatures of night,
The strength of my tides turns the edge of your mind,
That curtain once pulled back, such dark truths you'll find.

Such horror and sorrow and madness and pain,
The years that you drank are now pissed down Time's drain.
You are trapped in that morass called life where release
Is hidden from all who would seek swift surcease.

Just rock in your chair and nurse your old gun,
For the small hours are endless till daylight is won,
Can you make it once more till the first day of spring?
Through this tormenting darkness which winter must bring.

ODES AUTUMNAL

To Autumn

For Norma

There's a chill in the air which catches the heart,
Announcing October as warm days depart,
For greens turn to gold and wild sadness is hung
In scarlet and russet and purple and dun,
From hedgerows and woods for such glory is here
Which paints fading autumn in beauty, severe.
Almost too much to bear for the banks of the burn
Lie burnished with bronze as the fallen leaves turn.
The crystal brook chuckles as cool waters splash
Mid stones to still pools where the sun's late rays flash;
In dank secret glades poison fungi display
Vivid shades of corruption then liquid decay,
For this time is of dying of life's last etude
Where we learn about silence and lost solitude,
This waning of life hymns the year to its close
With forever's farewells to the loved in repose.
They may never return, they have lived out life's lease,
They must drift beyond Lethe in slumber and peace.
From life's loving cup so briefly we drink
Before we must all into the shadowed realms sink.
Winds moan in despair for the nights now grow long
Announcing All-Hallows, where lost spirits throng.
Yet the sad soul may soar for a moment at least
As eyes gladly gorge on this ravishing feast.
Constellations of colour paint mind-pallets bright

As morn lighted tints almost blind with delight.
Thus, my thoughts sing fulfilment at joy's gift, profound,
Seen through love's spectrum where wonders abound.
Though all things must pass this old season again
Will return in full splendour to lessen our pain,
For there's something immortal of autumn which says:
This vision revealed will be with you always,
Put grief far behind, greet this realm's ecstasy,
Then leave, unafraid of death's veiled mystery.

To Darkness and the Firelight

I sit in soft shadows as coals throw,
Their cheery delight round the room,
The devil-red warmth of the hearth's glow,
Dispels melancholy's black gloom.

I sit with my thoughts and the silence
A smooth golden malt in my hand
And wonder what waits in this year hence
And what fate's caprices have planned.

I ponder those lost in the darkness,
Those loved, nevermore to be seen,
I treasure their memories' sweet richness
Yet wonder what all endings mean.

Those thought seas I drift in—unfathomed!
Uncharted those deeps I explore.
The vessel I sail, dream provisioned.
To seek meaning on some far shore.

I call down delights, maledictions,
For whimsy alone steers my course,
Through reefs of half-truths and old fictions
Past where Sinbad sailed or the Norse

Or where bold Odysseus drifted
To fabled, lost, magical lands.
Where Cyclops and Sirens, mind-pictured,
Arise at my musings commands.

I sit here alone with the firelight
Adrift on my unique, strange, sea,
In comfort with Whisky at midnight,
And no better company than me.

To the Ending of Autumn

Till time dissolves in death's eternity
Each year will fill the woods with promise new.
With yearning shoots and green fecundity
As buds and blooms and fruits in turn pursue
Their need to ripen through September days,
Then hang, fulfilled, upon each drooping bough,
In late contentment, threading autumn ways
Till fitful winds pursue the trudging plough
Which breaks the stubbled rows, to brow the earth
With sullen furrows heaped with sodden clay.
Awaiting spring's new seeding and rebirth
Beyond this dank November's dull dismay.

While fading days decline those sad, limp leaves
Must tremble, pale, then join the raging flood
Of falling beauty as blithe autumn breathes.
Then cast of splendour fills the waiting wood,
Sickly yellows join the golden throng
Mixed with fevered reds and burning browns
Which rage, decay, through this year's evensong
As twilight welcomes barren trees where crows
Complain of emptied fields made bleak by frost,
Through nightfall all the world becomes morose
In dull cold realms where warmth and joy are lost.

Soon Proserpine descends to winter's tomb,
Then all my woods' immortal grandeur sleeps,
Life's flame bare flickers through this solstice gloom
For Sol's pale glow to slow extinction creeps.

Yet comfort in the warm coal fire still lives,
As I endure for now this profound night.
Hope of snowdrops some small comfort gives
And with it, spring's rebirth and living light.

To the Eternal Moon

Silent goddess of the night
You fill my world with silver light
Yoked by moments, paired, we glide,
Yet I alone awareness ride,
You above and I below
See what we see, know what we know.

You are forever, I am brief
You undiminished by that thief
Which steals all earthbound creatures' years
And leaves them full of pointless tears.
You above and I below
Do what we do, reap what we sow.

Brother, sister, bound by time,
I am mortal, you divine
You move through space in endless curves
For me just one short lifetime serves,
You above and I below,
I must cease while on you go.

For you time passes silently
You glide in beauty, you are free.
But I am bound by earthly chains,
How much tenure here remains?
You above and I below,
For me the flame of life burns low.

We vainly seek past meanings mask,
Our purpose here, a fool might ask!
We journey through the great unknown
My frailty soon must bear me home.
You above and I below
Through dreaming time my short years flow.

I live in turmoil, you in calm
You journey, graceful, free from harm
While I bear those ills, and blows
Which birth on all of man endows,
You above and I below,
A mortal's pain must always grow.

If you looked down and were aware
Would you voyage in despair?
Did nature damn us from the start?
Would it wish us to depart?
You above and I below
Just puppets in some shadow show.

New centuries our wars refresh
You must admit, we're good at death!
Millenia of practice now,
We all around this gift bestow.
You above and I below
And despair's voyage under-go.

Perhaps poetry may give us grace
Leave legacy of our poor race,
Shakespeare, Shelley might erase
Some portion of our kind's disgrace.
You above and I below,
I doubt our deeds will grace allow.

My mentors are Sardonic lords,
Poe and Swinburne guide these words
I grasp how near insanity
Aided their dark minstrelsy.
Them above and I below,
The hour is late, and I must go.

To Cynicism

Seconds, minutes, days glide by
Unstoppable, until you die
Unwelcome that appointed hour,
You may duck and dive and cower
But there is simply no escape
We waste our time we joke and jape,
Then, zap! You're gone and that is that,
There is no honorary lap.
When life's race is won, you're done,
A fate which waits each prince or bum.

Some believe in after lives!
A reason why religion thrives!
I would subscribe but for my doubt,
I see the dodgy ways they tout.
Their wares to save you via fees
To buy a place of endless ease
With milk and honey, angel wings
Those harps and other boring things.
No mention of a twelve-ale bar
Or race track or a sleek fast car,
Or hour glass blonds with pouty lips
Or redheads with Jayne Mansfield hips
Or smoky, smooth and golden malts
Matured an age in heaven's vaults.

I notice how they all get rich!
What they purvey, without a glitch,
Will fill their coffers, life's a dream
All promise, yet no proof is seen.
I wish that one gone past demise
Would send a card to say what lies
In that far beyond which waits,
What's found inside the Pearly Gates?
I'd pay the postage here collect
To find my cynic world view wrecked.
I feel that faith with such a proof
Would push attendance though the roof,
A promo vid of what it's like
In Hell could mend faith's leaking dyke
Which oozes stagnant, stale belief,
But what would that demise enfeoff?

A new more savage godly brand?
It's here already, ain't that grand,
A secularist state gone mad,
Like North K, but don't feel sad,
Perhaps the rational will emerge
As louder grows this death-wish dirge
Of creeds gone past their sell by date.
Somehow, I feel it's far too late
We teeter at the world's end brink
Into chaos we must sink.
Thus, watch your backs my feeble friends
As into madness all descends

117

To globalising greed and graft,
Haves and have nots, guile and craft
Much killing in the name of faith,
Human conscience, that poor wraith!

Maybe it's best to turn it in?
Do that though, the bastards win!
Thus, fight the fight until you're called,
Expect each hour to be appalled,
Yet rage against the dying light,
Hold out against eternal night
Until death's final coup d'etat
And your enforced, last, exeat.

To the Lowly Green

Only England, cool and damp,
Has this most peculiar stamp:
Everywhere is green.

All year the lawns, with odd dry patch,
If watered though these soon will match
And thus, are seldom seen.

The holly and the ivy, low,
All winter have a polished glow,
Though frosts are often keen.

Pine and larch and yew don't care,
They're richly garbed through Janu-aire,
For there they rule, supreme.

I don't forget the lowly moss
Which some dismiss as mouldy dross
In life's eternal scheme.

It plays its part to decorate
Forgotten tomb or rotting gate
With soft and gentle theme.

Fields, harvested are not brown long,
For winter shoots soon join the throng
Which spring's great lords convene.

Ancient fern fronds still abound
In varied forms they've been around
Since the Palaeocene.

I look askance at arid parts,
Where cactus grows and lizard darts,
And—cool waters seldom stream.

Give me thus this sceptre'd isle
Made evergreen by Puck's sweet guile
To gift midsummer's dream.

To the Fading of life

You're a fly-by-night flibbertigibbet,
A whimsical don't give a damn,
You take life as soon as you give it,
That surely is part of your plan.

Most float in your sea's upper reaches,
Plankton adrift on times stream,
Unknowing till death's writ impeaches
Their span with no notice; it's mean.

You may have some grandiose vision,
Of just how important you are,
Yet fate cuts your thread in derision,
Your deluded notions to mar.

Get nose into trough and then guzzle,
Go at it as hard as you may,
Grasp everything, but then you puzzle
Why does it all then slip away?

Some worry about the grim reaper
And build up a heavenly store –
Of promises, well they come cheaper
Than deep thought. Oh, that they abhor.

The good and the bad and the boring,
The stupid and wise genii,
Will all be released from life's whoring
Absolved from the need to ask why.

I glide through the sea of unknowing
And try to make sense of its tides,
I know that great currents are flowing,
Yet in them what secret resides?

The heart of this riddle eludes me,
I try but solutions won't come,
I sail towards night yet just don't see
What answers are there to be won.

The day closes soon, a last sunset.
I race but the vessel is old,
New futures will come, not for me I regret,
But for others their gifts will unfold.

To the Early Fifties

Those days were drab, and the world seemed cold,
The post-war world was weary, old,
Relieved, yet pinched with misery,
The whole house reeked of poverty.
Tobacco smoke was everywhere
Woodbine fumes filled all the air,
Dog ends littered asphalt streets,
Rationing still, there were no sweets!
Bomb shelters still at each house front
They smelled of pee and damp and want.

In kitchen stood an old stone sink
Trendy now, Belfast! wink, wink!
A coal fire burned there every day
Cooking smells never went away,
Crockery cracked and cutlery old
In short supply with little sold.

The table: twenties, made of deal,
We sat there for each spartan meal,
Covered by oil-cloth, threadbare cheap,
That working-class pre-plastic chic.

Fish and chips or a pint for a bob,
Twenty to a pound, each bloke had a job.
All seemed to work at Bullcroft pit.
Traders had a good life from it.
The row had a shoe shop, dress shop then,
Butchers to feed very hungry men

Who emerged from the mine with a hell of a thirst,
Eight boozers open, filled till they burst,
Two left now, they just survive
Showing Sky, in a place more dead than alive.
Now smack's to be had for the 'dopey' lads
The lasses all smoke the smuggled in fags.
On the shops now, six sell fast food,
Tattoos to be had, no bloody good!
If you have half a brain, you can see the con
You ain't improved when you get them done.

Back to the fifties, at that time:
No TV, just Big Ben's Chime
On the BBC for the news at nine.
Bobbies on the beat and we had little crime.

You could go to the flicks, changed twice a week,
Two films were showed, made very cheap.
The big ones came, like Gone With the Wind,
It took them years to reach our end.

There were few cars, but old horses came,
Ice cream, green grocers, coal in the rain
Which glistened and shone, it was dumped in the shed.
Very cheap, made so by mineworkers, dead.
Toiling down there, hundred-thousands then,
In a strength-made-world, made by strong men.
From steel and the mills and the great fishing fleets
Decimated now by EU cheats!

At the ends of the earth we might have been,
But the village life hummed though its streets were mean,
There was no dosh, but the war was won
With old ways dead and deference done,
Though some still stood when the picture screen
At the end of the film played 'God save the Queen'.
The old order, Church and Crown lay smashed.
Now crap is here, old values trashed,
Consumer trends and focus groups
Decide what's best, you jump through the hoops.

I had little time for that class riddled pageant
But do derive mirth from the 'heir apparent'
It's all gone now, just slow decline
And a sad ode penned to that far off time.

To the Sublime

What draught might quench a thirsting spirit's need?
As now the world dissolves in endless pain,
What cool and crystal waters will life cede
To sate our need and sanity regain.

Endless deserts stretch before us now
Into a future barren with despair,
Is there some Eden where hope's fruits will grow?
Does our nature call us to death's lair?

Will our species fill that Hall of Skulls?
As those gone before into time's mists.
Does judgement wait which all our crime annuls
Or just delusion in dream eucharists.

The die is cast perhaps, and we are done
And from the pit there may be no return.
Just endless mourning as doom's wage is won
For in this hell of greed we endless burn.

This earth around me seems to seek to show
Through small beauties all is not yet lost,
In pink last gleaming as the sun sinks low
Or magic written in the crystal frost.

Through dew drops hanging like some elvish tear,
Or flaming red and yellow leaves which fall
To herald autumn's glory late each year,
In woods which wait to share that sight with all.

It fills my heart to see the darting wren
Flit through the ivy, busy with her young,
That fragile sylph brings joy, again, again;
From stoic months her brief existence wrung.

Resting with the dogs when twilight comes,
I am content, my world is full, complete.
Slow moments with 'my wolves' beyond words sums
How simple pleasures make a life replete.

I feel the heartbeat of all life as one
Mid silent splendour, totally alone,
This lifts me from the gloom of Acheron
And fears of future days and paths unknown.

Though existence must for all decline
Into that dreadful abyss of lost light,
The music of the spheres still sounds, sublime,
When diamond stars encrust the velvet night.

To Proserpine

I dream of the Shades, of Proserpine
Of crystal nights, sublime,
Where mood and myths round midnight
In agony combine.

With Ceres long departed
Hades now must reign,
That black feast death has started
A guest there I remain.

My nightmares ride till morning
When wells of sleep are deep,
With memory sojourning
I must vigil keep.

Through weeks where despair taunts me
Till sunlight comes again,
Moon haunted, compelled, minstrelsy
Crafts verses half insane.

Of beauties' essence, dying,
A lyre forever still,
Of autumn's great goodbye-ing.
Death's god will have his will.

The world was green as Eden
Before despoilers came
They ploughed the un-trod meadow then,
And left raped wastes of shame.

That world green and virgin,
Through sacred groves life ran,
In innocence, yet urging
Fulfilment as youth can.

They danced to pipe and timbrel
In ecstasy and pain,
With rebirth as their symbol
They showed bleak death disdain.

Oh, where the pagan music?
Oh, where those dancers wild?
Oh, where that joy electric
Which innocents beguiled.

For leaves fall in the forest,
And shadows cloud the plain,
My spirit roams without a rest
Through kingdoms with no name.

Till torment's Queen can waken,
Put on her gown of lights
And leave this realm, forsaken,
To drink spring's new delights.

Yet think! Long days of pleasure,
Of plenty, soon must wane,
Soon dawn's soft mists will measure
How feeble Autumn's flame.

Once more I'll dream of Proserpine
Through velvet nights sublime,
Where mood and myths at midnight
In agony combine.

To the Moon

The mystic moon galleon moves stately and slow
With curling-wisp cloud waves beneath its great prow,
Its rigging is silver, it casts magic beams
On slumber locked lovers who drift in soft dreams.

It journeys in silence, lost times are its tides
For through countless aeons this dead vessel rides.
It scattered weak elf-light before man had come
Its pale glow will fall here long after he's gone.

It measures the ages as atoms decay
In orbit till doom falls upon the last day,
But now I must rise for its spell has me gripped
And write of this wonder with pen in ink dipped.

Its light 'ghosts' the graveyard and haunts the old hall
Then melts where first frost touch has pinched last leaf fall.
It peeps through the wild wood's gnarled Satan-black boughs
And fills secret hollows where dread death-cap grows.

It filigrees streamlets' quick flickers and swirls
Which lick smooth old pebbles in silent swift whorls.
Its spectre is welcome, it enters my room
To tame all dark terrors and banish the gloom.

My dog whines unease at these intruder gleams,
Through ice cold clear windows in magical beams.
That lantern must journey from dusk until dawn
New or in fullness, compelled and forlorn.

Can it be lonely? It looks so serene,
Virgin majestic, high midnight's dark queen.
Her voyage brings romance as Romeo found
He wooed Juliet by its occult orb bound.

Her witching-world secrets lie open at night
To all of love's fools bound in chains by moonlight.
Her minions are many, the bat and the owl
The slithering adder and timorous vole.

When mists sometimes veil her there's just a weak glow,
When skies are star brilliant her full beauties show,
Cuts swathes through those crepe skies which seep out from Hell
And banishes shadows where mind demons dwell.

Immortal she reigns while ephemerals we,
Drink deep of her lustre till dread destiny
Forecloses the lease on our short tenure here.
In death's long eclipse all our dreams disappear.

To a Walk down a Country Lane in Winter

With hedges bare my winding path
Turns through fields which feel the wrath
Of bleak post-solstice frozen blight,
For Boreas through burning lips
Breaths out that frost which cruelly grips
Vestigial day's first light.

Leaf piled mulch mounds in the ditch
Hold back those crystal waters which,
Clear midnight turns to ice.
Then sunlight, weak, just melts the gloom
Which shrouds this world, late afternoon
Might faltering warmth entice

From that low, wan, anaemic globe
Which louring clouds and mists enrobe
Through dreary winter hours.
Dead tussock-forts heap on the verge
Where crocus spears in green emerge
To promise early flowers.

On my left an empty wood
Where barren branches long to bud
And celebrate the spring.
But Janus will this urge en-chain
He knows two savage months remain
To bar life's hurrying.

Whilst on my right the streamlet's full,
Clear eddies form, dark currents pull
In wanton wild delight.
Round pebbles mossy fronds, with glee,
Dance and small whorls endlessly
Run downstream, in flight.

The paddock gate's a weathered grey
But rotting spars still hold at bay
Its patient, grazing, guests.
Through gentle eyes they watch me pace
My way through time and my small space
In search of those bequests,
Which come to me when deepest thought
With images I drink comport
Themselves to meld in verse.
This is my dark realm's rich reward
As snow makes white the sleeping sward
And word-dreams lift my curse.

To the Winter Solstice

Trees stand weeping bare and black,
Life's light is leached from day,
Hours pass slow each on the rack
Stretched out, full of dismay.

Through cloying dullness crept this dawn
No sunlight, just a shroud
Of clinging mist with dark thoughts born
Then to this hour endowed.

So foetid seems the heavy air
I take each poisoned breath,
This morning trudges through despair
And dreams of welcome death.

The shadow world will pass at noon
Marked by those ancient stones
That Henge reveals the path of doom
I feel it in my bones.

Now one o'clock the church bells chime
Those in their graves don't hear,
They sleep outside the realms of time
Beyond dark Lethe's mere.

Sad hours run slow, bleak twilight nears
Through murk and dismal gloom.
Enshrouding mist's soft veil of tears
Hangs mourning round my room.

Some light at last, it comes too late
For now dark crimson cloaks
Of cloud, fast-close eve's heaven's gate
And light's last gleaming chokes.

The Winter solstice, gods be praised,
Is past but time creeps slow
With longer days are spirits raised
And April's shoots soon show.

Yet now I face the longest night
I hope to meet the morn,
My soul's foul darkness must take flight
For soon bright Spring is born.

TO WINTER TWILIGHT

Fading twilight drifts through restful greys
As heavy veils wrap round the dying sun,
Now weary Rooks wing weary homeward ways,
Just slumber waits, the day's long work is done.

In nest and croft and burrow all must sleep
In warmth, in hope tomorrow will be kind.
For freezing winds might turn life's struggle bleak
Through frost bound fields where food is hard to find.

This hour is beauty though, a promise made
That all might yet be well, I wish it so
For all my brothers lodged in hedge and glade,
Snug innocents in nest and dark burrow.

Golds and silvers filigree the sky.
A final gleam the coming night defies,
As though this shaft of splendour might deny
The sad descent to gloaming as light dies.

The day ends in this evening gathering,
With hopes fulfilled and day's small purpose met
Or perhaps with hurt and wrongs still ravening,
Or sadness or with longing and regret.

Now burning reds turn sombre as the night
Puts out those final embers in the west,
There sullen clouds turn black as though some sprite
Has cast a spell which lays this eve to rest.

As darkness comes the tawny owl must rule,
Her realm will stretch from dusk until the dawn.
Through frost filled dells, above the icy pool,
She glides in silence till first hint of morn.

But cheering Yule logs light the solstice gloom,
Thus, from the dreary cold is comfort won.
As this year sinks to its forgotten tomb,
Just slumber waits, for now life's work is done.

To Winter's Music

Listen to Winter's music
As the sun gleams slant and low
When the old year's worn out lyric
Is fading sweet and low.

See the bright-eyed Blackbird, wary,
Pick the hawthorn's burning fruit
In these morning's dregs so weary
Through this month, born destitute.

How the frost-curled leaf wraiths shiver
When the chill-breeze stirs those hosts
Which in crumpled brown gowns quiver
As disintegrating ghosts.

There is green still, sickly moss grows
On old kerb and limestone wall
And sly ivy down old trees flows,
But bright holly crowns them all.

Shedding blood bright spots in mourning
For a world dissolved by time,
But my spirit soars sojourning
With these winter gifts sublime.

Here, impatient waits the dunnock
For first snowdrop-sign of spring,
But the wild skies promise havoc
And that dearth which north winds bring.

They must face the harsh weeks struggle
Hungry birds and fox and vole,
As in nest and lair they snuggle
But these bleak days take their toll.

But great nature's heart is beating
It will strengthen in the spring
As the new world wakes in greeting
To the bounties birth will bring.

Now I greet each frost white morning
When the air is clear and bright
For new hope grows with each dawning,
Soon the crocus brings delight.

To What was Lost

What was lost and what was won
On the road to Abaddon?
Last twilight comes, dawn fades away,
Life seemed to fill a single day.
Morning gifted: naïve youth,
I loved and sought eternal truth.
My teachers tried, what did I learn?
To question and let passions burn,
To stand alone and not conform,
To never settle for the norm.

Memories! When all was good
When need raged through young burning blood,
I stood in arrogance alone
Then strode into that great unknown
Of chances which my times bequeathed,
Which some would grasp through luck or need
Or boldness, I drank at that spring
And seized those gifts short years could bring.

My friends were few for I chose gods
Not weaker mortals, fools or clods
We had our day, but they are gone
Our band stood close with honours won.
We passed I think Life's sternest test
Uncompromising with the best.
Now I alone bear them with me
In mind, till falls eternity.

I looked for God, he was not there,
I trudged to evening in despair
And found just chaos, whims of fate,
And demons which will congregate
To prey on weakness which can thrive
When human lusts with greed connive,
Then those enslaved they will devour
With needs unsated hour on hour.

Love's fragile moments came my way,
What self-deluding games we play!
Those sin-filled, follied, dreams were sweet,
I, callow youth, thought all replete
But like brief blushes of first spring
All passions fade, pale hopes take wing,
Long buried mid those fleeting years
With heartache and those pointless tears.
The first faint star announces night
Has come, as fades the dying light;
I ponder long, I ponder slow
Still seeking, with that need to know
What purpose did existence bring?
Why death should be eternal king?
But I have lingered overlong
I hear the sighs of Abaddon.

To the Coming Light

Such weariness suffuses these small hours
Before first glimmers end this sullen dark
Which holds enfeebled days within its powers,
Till winter heads off in its shrouded barque,
To voyage through long shadows and despair.
Dark endings, death and desperate ennui
Now hold short solstice days within their lair
denying what sweet spring must soon set free.

Blithe snowdrops give the signal to begin
That bacchanal of rebirth and new joy,
Releasing floods of shoots whose burgeoning
Begins when Pan, life's ancient viceroy,
Commands the sun and south winds to conspire,
His pagan syrinx heard on every breeze,
To bring forth greening and that wild desire
Born mid the sacred southern Cyclades

And fill the world with pandemonium
Of verdure leaping through the days of May
To drink new warmth from an unconquered sun.
Yet sadness comes when falls midsummer's day,
For subtly come first signals of decline
For once again the world must turn to night.
But now wait months of beauty so sublime
Whilst swallows swoop, those deacons of delight.

Lightning Source UK Ltd.
Milton Keynes UK
UKHW03f1539290318
320234UK00001B/6/P